New Chinese for Children
新儿童汉语 ③

编著：刘 珣　张亚军　丁永寿
插图：赵倩倩　吴延明 等　英译：张 耘

Compiled by: Liu Xun
　　　　　　Zhang Yajun
　　　　　　Ding Yongshou

Illustrated by: Zhao Qianqian
　　　　　　　Wu Yanming et al.

Translated by: Zhang Yun

First Edition 2011

ISBN 978-7-5138-0084-6
Copyright 2011 by Sinolingua
Published by Sinolingua
24 Baiwanzhuang Road, Beijing 100037, China
Tel: (86)10-68320585,68997826
Fax: (86)10-68997826,68326333
http://www.sinolingua.com.cn
E-mail: hyjx@sinolingua.com.cn
Printed by Sanhe Huixin Printing Co., Ltd.

Printed in the People's Republic of China

致老师和家长们

《新儿童汉语》是为3～12岁的外国儿童学习汉语准备的初级读本。

本套教材分为三册，每册20课。第一册以语音为主，反复进行四声的基本功训练。第二、三册主要介绍汉语的一些基本句式，浅显易懂。每册后附有词汇表和辅导材料。词汇表收录的词语，遵循常用程度和重要性编排。辅导材料为中英文对照，对各课的语法点作了说明，是老师和家长的好帮手。

本套教材突出实用的原则，从儿童日常生活中最熟悉的事物入手，教给他们生活中使用最多的一些词汇，让他们学会说一些简单的生活用语。教材体现了较强的趣味性，选取儿童感兴趣的话题，反映儿童自己的生活。教材的主人公是中国和外国的孩子，内容上体现了儿童生活的特点，如课文中有游戏，小孩"过家家"，小兔、小狗、孙悟空，以及做梦到月亮上去旅行的情节等。

本套教材全部采用对话形式，并适当穿插一些谜语、儿歌、游戏、图画，形式活泼，语言生动，图文并茂。

学完这三册书后，小读者们能掌握300多个汉语词汇，以及一些最基本的语言材料，为将来系统、正规地学习汉语打下基础。

为了使您的孩子能准确地掌握发音，我们为本套教材配备了标准普通话录音光盘。

编者
2011年4月

To Teachers and Parents

New Chinese for Children is a series of elementary textbooks specifically designed to teach Chinese to children overseas who are three to twelve years old.

There are three books in all, each consisting of twenty lessons. Book 1 is aimed at teaching children correct Chinese pronunciation and the four tones through a wide range of pronunciation exercises; books 2 and 3 deal mainly with basic sentence patterns, all of which are simple and can be easily understood by children. Each book has an appendix that includes Teacher's Notes and a Vocabulary List. The Vocabulary List covers the key words used in daily communication by children. The bilingual Teacher's Notes explain the grammar points of each lesson and will be a useful guide for teachers and parents.

This series takes a practical approach to teaching, presenting the children with the familiar words and phrases that are most used in their everyday lives. The topics chosen will be interesting to children because they focus on a child's daily life; the leading characters in the books are all children, both Chinese and foreign, who talk about bunnies and doggies, games such as playing house, tell each other stories like the Monkey King and talk about the journeys they have taken to the moon in their dreams.

The texts are in the form of dialogues, and are enlivened by riddles, nursery rhymes, games and drawings. Lively language, together with a large number of illustrations, make this book appealing to children.

After completing this series, children will have a basic knowledge of the Chinese language that will include pronunciation, a vocabulary of over 300 words, and basic sentence patterns, which will lay a solid foundation for future Chinese language study.

To better help children in learning to pronounce Chinese correctly, we have included accompanying CDs to the texts.

The Compilers
April, 2011

Contents

1. 叔叔请进   1
2. 小小运动会   4
3. 打电话   7
4. 一件礼物   10
5. 讲故事   13
6. 北海公园   16
7. 坐电车   19
8. 去海边   22
9. 打扫教室   25
10. 咱们俩谁高?   28
11. 下来！下来！   31
12. 我帮你找哥哥   34
13. 你要买什么?   37
14. 娃娃病了   40
15. 找眼镜   43
16. 把电视打开   46
17. 冬冬的梦   49
18. 孙悟空飞来了   52
19. 你长大了做什么?   55
20. 新年好   58

词汇表   61

辅导材料   67

Teacher's Notes   71

1 叔叔请进

请 qǐng	please	坐 zuò	to sit	上班 shàngbān	to go to work
进 jìn	to come in, to enter	谢谢 xièxie	to thank, thank you	商店 shāngdiàn	shop
您 nín	you (polite form, singular)	家 jiā	home, family		

叔叔请进！
Uncle, please come in!

请坐！
Please sit down!

　　　谢谢。你爸爸在家吗？
　　　Thank you. Is your father in?

爸爸不在家。
No, he isn't.

　　　他去哪儿了？
　　　Where has he gone?

爸爸上班了。
He has gone to work.

　　　妈妈呢？
　　　What about your mother?

妈妈去商店了。
Mother has gone to the shop.

Shūshu qǐng jìn!

Qǐng zuò!

　　　Xièxie. Nǐ bàba zài jiā ma?

Bàba bú zài jiā.

　　　Tā qù nǎr le?

Bàba shàngbān le.

　　　Māma ne?

Māma qù shāngdiàn le.

Read aloud

阿姨好!

你好!你在做什么呢?

我玩儿呢。

你妈妈在家吗?

妈妈不在家。

她去哪儿了?

她去学校了。

你爸爸呢?

爸爸在家,阿姨请进!

Write sentences about what you see in the pictures

老师_____!

老师_____!

冬冬去哪儿了?

芳子去哪儿了?

2 小小运动会

运动会 sports meet yùndònghuì	跳高 high jump tiàogāo	跳 to jump tiào
昨天 yesterday zuótiān	赛跑 to run a race sàipǎo	高 high gāo
开（会） to have (a meeting) kāi（huì）	跑 to run pǎo	

爸爸，昨天我们开运动会了。
Dad, we had a sports meet yesterday.

你跳高了吗？
Did you take part in the high jump?

我没（有）跳高，
No, I didn't.

我赛跑了。
I ran a race.

谁跑得最快？
Who ran the fastest?

冬冬跑得最快。
Dongdong ran the fastest.

谁跳得最高？
Who jumped the highest?

兰兰跳得最高。
Lanlan jumped the highest.

Bàba, zuótiān wǒmen kāi yùndònghuì le.

Nǐ tiàogāo le ma?

Wǒ méi(yǒu) tiàogāo,

wǒ sàipǎo le.

Shuí pǎo de zuì kuài?

Dōngdong pǎo de zuì kuài.

Shuí tiào de zuì gāo?

Lánlan tiào de zuì gāo.

Read aloud

他们在做什么呢?

    他们在开运动会呢。

谁跑得最快?

    兔子跑得最快。

谁跳得最远（yuǎn, far）?

    青蛙（qīngwā, frog）跳得最远。

谁跳得最高?

    蚱蜢（zhàměng, grasshopper）跳得最高。

Write sentences about what you see in the pictures

昨天你们做什么了?

昨天你去学校了吗?

3 打电话

打（电话）dǎ(diànhuà)	to make (a phone call)	忙 máng	busy	能 néng	can, able to
喂 wèi	hello	电话 diànhuà	telephone	见 jiàn	to see
呀 ya	*modal particle*	明天 míngtiān	tomorrow		

喂，谁呀？
Hello? Who is it, please?

我是芳子。
This is Fangzi speaking.

你是玛丽吗？
Is that Mary speaking?

我是玛丽。
Yes, it is.

你好，玛丽。
Hello, Mary.

你忙不忙？
Are you busy?

我不忙。
I'm not busy.

明天是我的生日。
It's my birthday tomorrow.

你能不能来我家？
Can you come to my house?

能。
Yes, I can.

好，明天见。
OK. See you tomorrow.

明天见。
See you tomorrow.

Wèi, shuí ya?

Wǒ shì Fāngzǐ.

Nǐ shì Mǎlì ma?

Wǒ shì Mǎlì.

Nǐ hǎo, Mǎlì.

Nǐ máng bù máng?

Wǒ bù máng.

Míngtiān shì wǒ de shēngrì.

Nǐ néng bù néng lái wǒ jiā?

Néng.

Hǎo, míngtiān jiàn.

Míngtiān jiàn.

Read aloud

喂?

您好,阿姨。兰兰在家吗?

兰兰不在家,你是谁呀?

我是冬冬。阿姨,兰兰去哪儿了?

她去天安门了。

她今天去不去学校?

今天是星期日,她不去学校。

您能不能告诉(gàosu, to tell)她,明天八点半开运动会。

好,谢谢你。

不谢。阿姨再见。

再见。

Write sentences about what you see in the pictures

_____?
(写不写)

_____?
(穿不穿)

_____?
(要不要)

_____?
(有没有)

4 一件礼物

礼物 lǐwù	present	祝 zhù	to wish, to congratulate	糖 táng	sweets, candy
蛋糕 dàngāo	cake	送 sòng	to give (a present)	金鱼 jīnyú	goldfish
听 tīng	to listen	猜 cāi	to guess	大 dà	big, old

听，冬冬来了。
Listen, here comes Dongdong.

芳子，祝你生日好！
Happy birthday, Fangzi!

谢谢。
Thank you.

我送你一件礼物。
Here is a present for you.

什么礼物？
What is it?

你猜。
Have a guess.

是大蛋糕。对不对？
It's a big cake. Right?

不对。
No.

是糖？
Candy?

也不对。
Wrong again.

你看，这是什么？
Look, what is it?

小金鱼！
Little goldfish!

Tīng, Dōngdong lái le.

Fāngzǐ, zhù nǐ shēngrì hǎo!

Xièxie.

Wǒ sòng nǐ yí jiàn lǐwù.

Shénme lǐwù?

Nǐ cāi.

Shì dà dàngāo. Duì bu duì?

Bú duì.

Shì táng?

Yě bú duì.

Nǐ kàn, zhè shì shénme?

Xiǎo jīnyú!

Read aloud

今天是妈妈的生日,爸爸、哥哥(gēge)、妹妹(mèimei)都给(gěi)妈妈一件礼物。爸爸送妈妈一件毛衣,哥哥送妈妈一个生日蛋糕,妹妹送妈妈一盒(hé, box)糖。小红给妈妈什么呢?她画了一张画儿,上面有很多花儿,还写了六个字:"祝妈妈生日好!"

Write sentences about what you see in the pictures

他送阿姨什么?
_____。

谁送玛丽一只小鸟?
_____。

奶奶给她什么?
_____。

芳子教谁《新儿童汉语》?
_____。

5 讲故事

讲 jiǎng	to tell	给 gěi	for, to	过 guo	aspectual particle
故事 gùshi	story	以前 yǐqián	ago, before	乌龟 wūguī	tortoise
爷爷 yéye	grandpa	电影 diànyǐng	film	孙悟空 Sūn Wùkōng	the Monkey King

老爷爷，您给我们讲个故事，好吗？
Grandpa, please tell us a story.

好。很早很早以前，
All right. Once upon a time,

有一只小兔和一只小乌龟……
there was a hare and a tortoise ...

这个故事我们听过了。
We have heard this story.

很早很早以前，
Once upon a time,

有一只小羊……
there was a little lamb ...

这个，我们也看过电影了。
We have seen this film, too.

你们喜欢听什么呢？
What do you like listening to?

我们最喜欢听孙悟空的故事。
We like to listen to the story of the Monkey King best.

Lǎoyéye, nín gěi wǒmen jiǎng ge gùshi, hǎo ma?

Hǎo. Hěn zǎo hěn zǎo yǐqián,

yǒu yì zhī xiǎo tù hé yì zhī xiǎo wūguī...

Zhège gùshi wǒmen tīngguo le.

Hěn zǎo hěn zǎo yǐqián,

yǒu yì zhī xiǎo yáng...

Zhège, wǒmen yě kànguo diànyǐng le.

Nǐmen xǐhuan tīng shénme ne?

Wǒmen zuì xǐhuan tīng Sūn Wùkōng de gùshi.

Read aloud

老师好！老师，你给我们讲一个故事吧。

你们喜欢听什么故事呢？

我喜欢小白兔的故事。

不好，不好。我要听孙悟空的故事。

孙悟空的故事老师讲过了。

我给你们讲"渔夫（yúfū, fisherman）和金鱼"的故事吧。

Write sentences about what you see in the pictures

芳子去过天安门吗？

_____。

你学过这个汉字吗？

_____。

谁在给娃娃穿衣服呢？

_____。

冬冬在给谁打电话呢？

_____。

6 北海公园

北海公园 Běihǎi Gōngyuán	Beihai Park	湖 hú	lake	船 chuán	boat, ship
山 shān	hill	划 huá	to row	爬 pá	to climb
还 hái	as well	跟 gēn	with	一起 yìqǐ	together

玛丽，你去过北海公园吗？
Have you ever been
to Beihai Park, Mary?

没有去过。
No, I haven't.

北海公园里有山吗？
Is there a hill in Beihai Park?

有山，还有湖。
Yes, and there is a lake as well.

在那儿能划船吗？
Can people go rowing there?

能，我在那儿划过船，
Yes, I've been rowing there,

还爬过山。
and I've climbed the hill, too.

星期天你跟我们一起去，好吗？
Will you go with us on Sunday?

好。
Certainly.

Mǎlì, nǐ qùguo Běihǎi Gōngyuán ma?

Méiyǒu qùguo.

Běihǎi Gōngyuán li yǒu shān ma?

Yǒu shān, háiyǒu hú.

Zài nàr néng huá chuán ma?

Néng, wǒ zài nàr huáguo chuán,

hái páguo shān.

Xīngqītiān nǐ gēn wǒmen yìqǐ qù, hǎo ma?

Hǎo.

Read aloud

北京有一个很大的公园，叫北海公园。公园里有山，有湖，山上还有一个白塔 (tǎ, pagoda)。那儿的树和花儿真多，小鸟在树上唱歌，蝴蝶 (húdié, butterfly) 在花儿里跳舞。

冬冬最喜欢北海公园。星期天，他跟爸爸、妈妈在公园里划船。冬冬划船划得很好，爬山也爬得很快，他们玩得真高兴 (gāoxìng, happy)。

Write sentences about what you see in the pictures

他在哪儿游泳？

他在＿＿＿＿＿＿里游泳。

他们在哪儿听故事？

他们在＿＿＿＿＿＿里听故事。

她跟谁一起滑冰？

她跟＿＿＿＿＿＿一起滑旱冰。

他跟谁一起看电影？

他跟＿＿＿＿＿＿一起看电影。

7 坐电车

电车 diànchē	tram	张 zhāng	*measure word*	车 chē	vehicle
买 mǎi	to buy	到 dào	to go to, to arrive	要 yào	will, to be going to
票 piào	ticket	吧 ba	*modal particle*	下 xià	to get off

请买票。
Fares, please.

    阿姨，买三张（票）。
    Auntie, three tickets, please.

到哪儿？
Where to?

    北海公园。
    Beihai Park.

    老爷爷，您坐这儿吧。
    Grandpa, please sit here.

好孩子，谢谢你们。
You're good children, thank you.

    不谢。
    Not at all.

    ... ...

    北海要到了，
    We're almost at Beihai.

    老爷爷，我们要下车了。
    Grandpa, we're going to get off the tram.

    再见。
    Goodbye.

再见。
Bye-bye.

Qǐng mǎi piào.

    Āyí, mǎi sān zhāng piào.

Dào nǎr?

    Běihǎi Gōngyuán.

    Lǎoyéye, nín zuò zhèr ba.

Hǎo háizi, xièxie nǐmen.

    Bú xiè.

    ... ...

Běihǎi yào dào le,

lǎoyéye, wǒmen yào xià chē le.

    Zàijiàn.

Zàijiàn.

Read aloud

阿姨，去动物园（dòngwùyuán, the zoo）坐几路（jǐ lù, which number) 车？

　　坐103路电车。

谢谢您。

　　不谢。

叔叔，买票。

　　到哪儿？

到动物园。

　　买几张？

两张。

Write sentences about what you see in the pictures

车还没有来吗？
车＿＿＿＿＿＿了。

北海到了。
快，我们要＿＿＿＿＿＿了。

快跑！
要＿＿＿＿＿＿了。

今天真冷。
要＿＿＿＿＿＿了。

8 去海边

海边 hǎi biān	seaside	旅行 lǚxíng	to travel	火车 huǒchē	train
放（假） fàng (jià)	to have (a holiday)	哥哥 gēge	elder brother	第 dì	ordinal prefix (-st, -nd, -rd)
暑假 shǔjià	summer holiday, summer vacation	怎么 zěnme	how	次 cì	time

快要放暑假了。
The summer holidays is coming.

暑假你去哪儿旅行?
Where are you going to go during the holiday?

 我去海边旅行。
 I'm going to the seaside.

你跟谁一起去?
Whom are you going to go with?

 我跟爸爸、妈妈、哥哥一起去。
 With my father, mother, and elder brother.

你们怎么去?
How are you going to go there?

 我们坐火车去。
 By train.

你以前去过海边吗?
Have you ever been to the seaside?

 没有,这是第一次。
 No. This is the first time.

祝你玩得好。
Have a good time.

Kuài yào fàng shǔjià le.

Shǔjià nǐ qù nǎr lǚxíng?

 Wǒ qù hǎi biān lǚxíng.

Nǐ gēn shuí yìqǐ qù?

 Wǒ gēn bàba, māma, gēge yìqǐ qù.

Nǐmen zěnme qù?

 Wǒmen zuò huǒchē qù.

Nǐ yǐqián qùguo hǎi biān ma?

 Méiyǒu, zhè shì dì-yī cì.

Zhù nǐ wánr de hǎo.

Read aloud

寒假（hánjià, winter holiday, winter vacation）到了，玛丽的爷爷和奶奶（nǎinai）要来中国旅行，他们先坐飞机（fēijī）到广州（Guǎngzhōu）。爸爸和玛丽也去广州，跟爷爷、奶奶一起坐火车到北京。

爷爷和奶奶以前来过中国，他们没有到过北京。这一次，玛丽要跟他们去长城（Chángchéng）玩儿，还要去北海、天安门（Tiān'ānmén），她要给爷爷、奶奶讲很多的中国故事。

Write sentences about what you see in the pictures

他去公园干什么？
_____。

妈妈去商店买什么？
_____。

_____？
他骑自行车去学校。

_____？
她坐电车上班。

9 打扫教室

打扫 to clean dǎosǎo	咱们 we, us zánmen	窗户 window chuānghu	开始 to begin, to start kāishǐ
教室 classroom jiàoshì	擦 to wipe cā	用 to use yòng	
脏 dirty zāng	椅子 chair yǐzi	抹布 rag mābù	

教室里真脏，
The classroom is very dirty.

咱们打扫打扫，好吗？
Shall we clean it?

　　好。我做什么呢？
　　Yes. What shall I do?

你擦桌子和椅子。
You wipe the desks and chairs.

我来擦窗户。
I will clean the windows.

　　我用什么擦桌子呢？
　　What shall I wipe the desks with?

你用抹布。
With a rag.

看，那儿有抹布。
Look, there are some rags.

　　咱们开始吧。
　　Let's begin.

Jiàoshì li zhēn zāng,

zánmen dǎsǎo dǎsǎo, hǎo ma?

　　Hǎo. Wǒ zuò shénme ne?

Nǐ cā zhuōzi hé yǐzi.

Wǒ lái cā chuānghu.

　　Wǒ yòng shénme cā zhuōzi ne?

Nǐ yòng mābù.

Kàn, nàr yǒu mābù.

　　Zánmen kāishǐ ba.

Read aloud

今天是星期天，爸爸、妈妈起得很早，他们在打扫屋子呢。哥哥说："弟弟，快起床！咱们也打扫打扫吧，屋子太脏了。"弟弟说："我不，我不，星期天我还想多睡（shuì）一会儿呢！"

哥哥开始打扫了，他用抹布擦窗户、擦桌子和椅子，还擦了地板（dìbǎn, floor）。

十点半，弟弟起床了。他看看这儿，看看那儿，屋里真干净（gānjìng, clean）。

小猫（māo）看见弟弟，miāomiāo叫。小猫在说："懒，懒，你真懒！"

Write sentences about what you see in the pictures

你会写这个汉字吗？

我_____。（想）

他用什么吃饭？

_____。

10 咱们俩谁高？

比 bǐ	to compare, than	奶奶 nǎinai	grandma	一点儿 yìdiǎnr	a little
俩 liǎ	two; both	过（来）guò (lai)	to come (here)	胖 pàng	fat, chubby
当然 dāngrán	of course	矮 ǎi	short	还是 háishi	or

咱们俩谁高？
Let's see who is taller, you or I?

 当然我比你高。
 Of course, I'm taller than you.

我比你高。
I'm taller than you.

奶奶，您说谁高？
Grandma,
please tell us who is taller?

 过来，我看看。冬冬比你高。
 Come here, let me see.
 Dongdong is taller than you.

 你比冬冬矮一点儿。
 You are a little shorter than
 Dongdong.

我胖还是冬冬胖？
Who is chubbier,
Dongdong or I?

 你比冬冬胖。
 You are chubbier than
 Dongdong.

Zánmen liǎ shuí gāo?

 Dāngrán wǒ bǐ nǐ gāo.

Wǒ bǐ nǐ gāo.

Nǎinai, nín shuō shuí gāo?

 Guòlai, wǒ kànkan.
 Dōngdong bǐ nǐ gāo.

 Nǐ bǐ Dōngdong ǎi
 yìdiǎnr.

Wǒ pàng háishi
Dōngdong pàng?

 Nǐ bǐ Dōngdong pàng.

Read aloud

冬冬大（dà, old）还是玛丽大？
　　当然玛丽比冬冬大。
玛丽比冬冬大几岁？
　　玛丽比冬冬大一岁。
今天玛丽忙还是冬冬忙？
　　冬冬比玛丽忙。冬冬今天要赛跑，还要跳高。

Write sentences about what you see in the pictures

小兔子快还是小乌龟快？
_____比_____。

冬冬早还是芳子早？
_____比_____。

哥哥的屋子脏还是弟弟的屋子脏？
_____比_____。

今天冷还是昨天冷？
_____比_____。

11 下来！下来！

干 gàn	to do	上 shàng	to come up	老鼠 lǎoshǔ	mouse
告诉 gàosu	to tell	出 chū	to come out	后来 hòulái	later
事 shì	thing	捉 zhuō	to catch	可惜 kěxī	it's a pity

山姆，下来！下来！
Sam, get down! Get down!

干什么？
Why?

告诉你一件事。
I've got somthing to tell you.

你上来吧。
You come up.

不，你下来吧。快点儿出来！
No, you come down. Come out at once!

什么事？
What is it?

我的小狗捉了一只大老鼠。
My puppy caught a big mouse.

真的吗？
Really?

后来老鼠跑了。
But later, the mouse ran away.

真可惜！
What a pity!

Shānmǔ, xiàlai! xiàlai!

Gàn shénme?

Gàosu nǐ yí jiàn shì.

Nǐ shànglai ba.

Bù, nǐ xiàlai ba. Kuàidiǎnr chūlai!

Shénme shì?

Wǒ de xiǎo gǒu zhuōle yì zhī dà lǎoshǔ.

Zhēnde ma?

Hòulái, lǎoshǔ pǎo le.

Zhēn kěxī!

Read aloud

兰兰在家吗？

　　在，快进来。

兰兰，你看这个书包好不好？

　　真好。你昨天去商店了吗？

我昨天去商店了。

　　你还买什么了？

我还买了两支笔和三张画儿。

Write sentences about what you see in the pictures

请 _____ 来！

_____ 来！你看这是什么？

你 _____ 来，我告诉你一件事。

你们快 _____ 来，这儿真好。

12 我帮你找哥哥

帮 bāng	to help	妹妹 mèimei	younger sister	让 ràng	to let
找 zhǎo	to look for	哭 kū	to cry, to weep	等 děng	to wait
回 huí	to go back	还 hái	still		

小妹妹，你哭什么？
Why are you crying, little sister?

哥哥去买苹果了，
My elder brother has gone to get some apples.

他让我等他。
He asked me to wait for him.

他还不回来。
But he still has not come back.

我帮你找哥哥好吗？
I'll help you look for your elder brother, all right?

好。
All right.

看，谁来了？
Look, who's coming?

哥哥，哥哥！
Brother, brother!

Xiǎo mèimei, nǐ kū shénme?

Gēge qù mǎi píngguǒ le.

Tā ràng wǒ děng tā,

tā hái bù huílai.

Wǒ bāng nǐ zhǎo gēge hǎo ma?

Hǎo.

Kàn, shuí lái le?

Gēge, gēge!

Read aloud

今天是儿童节（Értóngjié, Children's Day）。冬冬请玛丽、芳子和山姆到他家玩儿。冬冬的爸爸买了四张电影票，请他们去看电影。看什么电影呢？冬冬让他们猜。山姆想了想说："是《熊猫商店》。"芳子说："是《小蝌蚪（kēdǒu, tadpole）找妈妈》。"冬冬告诉他们，猜得都不对，是《三毛（Sānmáo, a person's name）的故事》。

Write sentences about what you see in the pictures

那儿有一个公园，
咱们_____去看看吧。

他们在山上呢，
咱们也_____去，好吗？

咱们快_____去吧。

他们呢？
他们都_____去了。

13 你要买什么?

售货员 shòuhuòyuán	shop assistant	钱 qián	money	加 jiā	plus
小朋友 xiǎopéngyǒu	child, kid	算 suàn	to reckon, to add up	对不起 duìbuqǐ	sorry
本子 běnzi	exercise book	毛 máo	mao	块 kuài	*measure word*
多少 duōshao	how much, how many	没关系 méi guānxi	that's all right, it doesn't matter		

售货员叔叔，您好！
Hello, Uncle (shop assistant)!

你好，小朋友。
Hello, kid.

你要买什么？
Can I help you?

两个本子，一支笔。
I want two exercise books and a pencil.

好的。
OK.

多少钱？
How much is that?

我算算：一块一加一块二是两块二。
Let me see. One yuan and one *jiao* plus one yuan and two *jiao* is two yuan and two *jiao*.

不对，不对。我帮你算。
That's not right. Let me help you.

一块一加一块二是两块三。
One yuan and one *jiao* plus one yuan and two *jiao* is two yuan and three *jiao*.

对不起。
I am sorry.

没关系。
That's all right.

Shòuhuòyuán shūshu, nín hǎo !

Nǐ hǎo, xiǎopényǒu.

Nǐ yào mǎi shénme?

Liǎng gè běnzi, yì zhī bǐ.

Hǎode.

Duōshao qián?

Wǒ suànsuan:yí kuài yī jiā yí kuài èr shì liǎng kuài èr.

Bú duì,bú duì. Wǒ bāng nǐ suàn.

Yí kuài yī jiā yí kuài èr shì liǎng kuài sān.

Duìbuqǐ.

Méi guānxi.

Read aloud

妈妈让弟弟买五个本子、两支笔和一个面包。一个本子是五毛五分（fēn, fen）钱，五个本子是两块七毛五。一支笔是一块二毛钱，两支笔是两块四。一个面包是六块五。请你帮弟弟算算，他今天用了多少钱？（一块 = 十毛 = 一百分，one yuan = ten mao = one hundered fen）

两块七毛五加两块四是五块一毛五，五块一毛五加六块五是十一块六毛五。对！他用了十一块六毛五。

Write sentences about what you see in the pictures

对不起！
没关系。

_____。
_____。

你要_____？
我要_____。

你要_____？
我要_____。

14 娃娃病了

病 bìng	to be ill	咳嗽 késou	to cough	怕 pà	to be afraid
大夫 dàifu	doctor	发烧 fāshāo	to have a fever	药 yào	medicine
舒服 shūfu	well, comfortable	打针 dǎzhēn	to have an injection	天 tiān	day
疼 téng	ache, pain				

娃娃怎么了？
What's the matter with the doll?

　　大夫，娃娃生病了。
　　Doctor, the doll is ill.

她哪儿不舒服？
What's wrong with her?

　　她头疼、咳嗽。
　　She has a headache and she is coughing.

发烧不发烧？
Has she got a fever?

　　发烧。
　　Yes, she has.

给她打针吧。
Let's give her an injection.

　　不，她怕打针。
　　No, she's afraid of injections.

吃点药，好吗？
Will she take some medicine?

　　好。
　　Yes.

一天吃三次。
It is to be taken three times a day.

Wáwa zěnme le?

　　Dàifu, wáwa bìng le.

Tā nǎr bù shūfu?

　　Tā tóu téng, késou.

Fāshāo bu fāshāo?

　　Fāshāo.

Gěi tā dǎzhēn ba.

　　Bù, tā pà dǎzhēn.

Chī diǎnr yào, hǎo ma?

　　Hǎo.

Yì tiān chī sān cì.

Read aloud

昨天是星期天，冬冬跟小朋友们在外边滑冰。他们玩儿了半天。

冬冬今天没有起床。他头疼、咳嗽，很不舒服。妈妈给他做了面条（miàntiáo, noodles），他也不想吃。爸爸请大夫给他看病（kànbìng, to examine a patient），大夫说：冬冬感冒（gǎnmào, catch a cold）了。他给冬冬打针，给他吃药。大夫让冬冬在家休息（xiūxi, to rest）两天。

Write sentences about what you see in the pictures

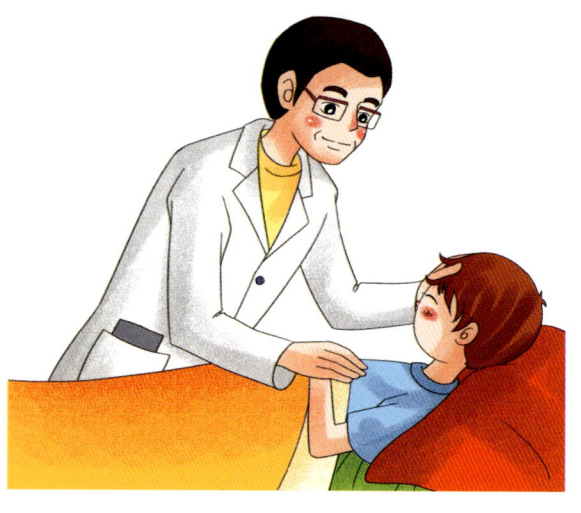

15 找眼镜

眼镜 yǎnjìng	glasses	复习 fùxí	to review	练习 liànxí	exercise
放 fàng	to put	功课 gōngkè	lesson	刚才 gāngcái	just now
忘 wàng	to forget	完 wán	to finish	啊 à	oh
不用 búyòng	need not				

奶奶，您在找什么？
Grandma, what are you looking for?

   我在找眼镜。
   I'm looking for my glasses.

您放在哪儿了？
Where did you leave them?

   我忘了。
   I've forgotten.

我帮您找。
Let me help you.

   不用了，你快去复习功课吧。
   There's no need. You must hurry and review your lessons.

我复习完了，也做完练习了。
I've finished reviewing my lessons, and I've done my exercises.

奶奶，您今天用眼镜了吗？
Grandma, did you use your glasses today?

   刚才用了。
   I used them just now.

您头上是什么？
What's on your head?

   啊，找到了。
   Oh, here they are.

Nǎinai, nín zài zhǎo shénme?

   Wǒ zài zhǎo yǎnjìng.

Nín fàng zài nǎr le?

   Wǒ wàng le.

Wǒ bāng nín zhǎo.

   Búyòng le, nǐ kuài qù fùxí gōngkè ba.

Wǒ fùxí wán le, yě zuòwán liànxí le.

Nǎinai, nín jīntiān yòng yǎnjìng le ma?

   Gāngcái yòng le.

Nín tóu shang shì shénme?

   À, zhǎodào le.

Read aloud

　　玛丽给兰兰打了一个电话，她要兰兰跟她一起出去玩儿。兰兰正在家里做练习题呢。她告诉玛丽，她很忙，做完练习题还要复习功课，今天不能去了。兰兰问玛丽，昨天开运动会，丢（diū, to lose）的帽子（màozi, hat）找到没有。玛丽说没有，刚才去商店，想买一个帽子，可是（kěshì, but）没有买到。兰兰跟玛丽说，明天她们一起去商店看看。

Write sentences about what you see in the pictures

16 把电视打开

把 bǎ	preposition showing disposal	节目 jiémù	programme	门 mén	door
电视 diànshì	TV	月亮 yuèliang	the moon	关 guān	to close
打（开） dǎ (kāi)	to turn on, to open	太 tài	too, very		
开 kāi	to open	睡觉 shuìjiào	to go to bed		

妈妈，我想看电视。
Mum, I want to watch TV.

你做完数学作业了吗？
Have you finished your math exercises?

做完了。
Yes, I have.

今天的汉字你都写对了吗？
Have you copied today's Chinese characters correctly?

写对了。
Yes.

好吧，你把电视打开。
All right, turn on the TV then.

今天有什么节目？
What programme is on today?

今天有"去月亮上旅行"。
Today *A trip to the Moon* is on.

太好了！
That's wonderful!

看完了，你把门关上，早点儿睡觉。
Close the door after you have finished watching TV. Go to bed early.

好。
OK.

Māma, wǒ xiǎng kàn diànshì.

Nǐ zuòwán shùxué zuòyè le ma?

Zuòwán le.

Jīntiān de Hànzì nǐ dōu xiěduì le ma?

Xiěduì le.

Hǎo ba, nǐ bǎ diànshì dǎkāi.

Jīntiān yǒu shénme jiémù?

Jīntiān yǒu *Qù Yuèliang Shang Lǚxíng*.

Tài hǎo le!

Kànwán le, nǐ bǎ mén guānshang, zǎo diǎnr shuìjiào.

Hǎo.

Read aloud

六点多了,弟弟还在复习功课呢。他想快点儿把功课复习完,七点钟看电视。今天有好节目——足球(zúqiú, football)赛。弟弟最喜欢看足球赛。

妈妈进来了。她看见弟弟在复习,说:"天黑了,快把灯(dēng, light)打开!"

七点钟,弟弟把灯关上,把电视打开。

Write sentences about what you see in the pictures

请你把门_____。

请你把电视机_____。

把窗户_____,好吗?

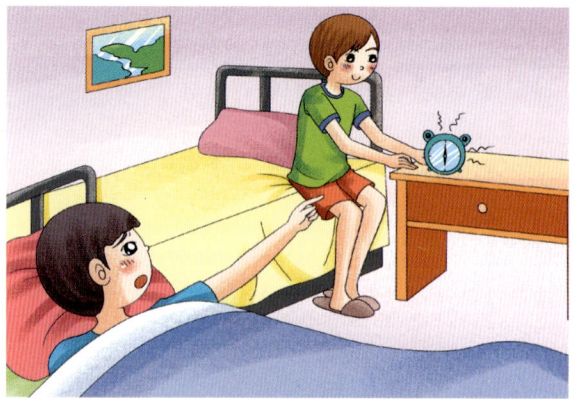

把收音机(shōuyīnjī, radio)
_____,好吗?

17 冬冬的梦

梦 mèng	dream	特别 tèbié	special	送 sòng	to take sb. to
宇航员 yǔhángyuán	astronaut	戴 dài	to wear	嫦娥 Cháng'é	Fairy Chang'e
飞船 fēichuán	spaceship	帽子 màozi	hat	高兴 gāoxìng	happy
着 zhe	particle indicating continuous action			轰 hōng	boom

看，那两个宇航员是谁？
Look, who are those two astronauts?
　　那是冬冬和玛丽。
　　That's Dongdong and Mary.
　　他们坐在飞船里。
　　They are sitting in a spaceship.
他们身上穿着什么呢？
What kind of clothes are they wearing?
　　他们身上穿着特别的衣服。
　　They are wearing special clothes.
他们头上戴着什么呢？
What kind of hats are they wearing?
　　他们戴着特别的帽子。
　　They are wearing special hats.
飞船把他们送到哪儿去？
Where is the spaceship taking them?
　　飞船把他们送上月亮。
　　The spaceship is carrying them to the moon.
他们去月亮上做什么？
What are they going to do on the moon?
　　他们去看嫦娥和小白兔。
　　They want to see Fairy Chang'e and the white rabbit.
　　他们真高兴。
　　They are very happy.
十、九、八、七、六、五、四、三、二、一。
Ten, nine, eight, seven, six, five, four, three, two, one.
　　轰！　Boom!

Kàn, nà liǎng gè yǔhángyuán shì shuí?

　　Nà shì Dōngdong hé Mǎlì.
　　Tāmen zuò zài fēichuán li.
Tāmen shēn shang chuānzhe shénme ne?

　　Tāmen shēn shang chuānzhe tèbié de yīfu.
Tāmen tóu shang dàizhe shénme ne?

　　Tāmen dàizhe tèbié de màozi.
Fēichuán bǎ tāmen sòngdào nǎr qù?

　　Fēichuán bǎ tāmen sòngshàng yuèliang.

Tāmen qù yuèliang shang zuò shénme?

　　Tāmen qù kàn Cháng'é hé xiǎo bái tù.

　　Tāmen zhēn gāoxìng.

Shí, jiǔ, bā, qī, liù, wǔ, sì, sān, èr, yī.

Hōng!

Read aloud

《去月亮上旅行》是一个很好的电视节目，小朋友们都喜欢看。有两个小宇航员和一只小狗，他们坐着飞船到月亮上旅行。

冬冬特别喜欢这个节目，他也想做一个宇航员。他看完电视，就（jiù, then）上床睡觉。他做了一个梦……

你看，屋子里灯还开着，桌子上放着他的汉字本。他穿着衣服睡在那儿。

Write sentences about what you see in the pictures

她穿着什么衣服？

_____。

桌子上放着什么？

_____。

纸上画着什么？

_____。

他戴着什么帽子？

_____。

18 孙悟空飞来了

飞 fēi	to fly	为什么 wèi shénme	why	长 cháng	long
地球 dìqiú	the earth	它 tā	it	所以 suǒyǐ	so, therefore
长城 Chángchéng	the Great Wall	因为 yīnwèi	because, for	拿 ná	to hold, to take
				桃子 táozi	peach

玛丽，你看见地球了吗？
Mary, have you seen the earth?

看见了。地球上是什么？
Yes. What's that there on the earth?

那是中国的长城。
It's the Great Wall of China.

为什么叫它长城？
Why is it called the Great Wall?

因为它很长，所以叫长城。
It's called the Great Wall because it is very long.

冬冬，你看谁飞来了？
Dongdong, look, who is flying towards us?

啊，孙悟空飞来了。
Oh, it's the Monkey King.

他手里拿着什么？
What is in his hand?

他手里拿着一个大桃子。
He is holding a peach.

孙悟空，您好！
Hello, Monkey King!

你也去月亮吗？
Are you going to the moon, too?

是的，我把桃子送给嫦娥。
Yes, I'm going to give the peach to Fairy Chang'e.

Mǎlì, nǐ kànjiàn dìqiú le ma?

Kànjiàn le. Dìqiú shang shì shénme?

Nà shì Zhōngguó de Chángchéng.

Wèi shénme jiào tā Chángchéng?

Yīnwèi tā hěn cháng, suǒyǐ jiào Chángchéng.

Dōngdong, nǐ kàn shuí fēilai le?

À, Sūn Wùkōng fēilai le.

Tā shǒu li názhe shénme?

Tā shǒu li názhe yí gè dà táozi.

Sūn Wùkōng, nín hǎo!

Nǐ yě qù yuèliang ma?

Shì de, wǒ bǎ táozi sòng gěi Cháng'é.

Read aloud

爷爷给冬冬讲过孙悟空和嫦娥的故事。孙悟空是一个猴子（hóuzi, monkey），因为他很勇敢（yǒnggǎn, brave），所以小朋友们都特别喜欢他。孙悟空飞得很快，比飞船还快。他为什么把桃子送给嫦娥呢？因为他自己很喜欢吃桃子。

嫦娥是一个仙女（xiānnǚ, fairy），她跟小白兔一起住（zhù, to live）在月亮上。

Write sentences about what you see in the pictures

为什么叫它长城？
_____。

冬冬为什么坐飞船？
_____。

他手里拿着什么书？
_____。

她戴着什么手套儿（shǒutàor）？
_____。

19 你长大了做什么？

长 zhǎng	to grow	非洲 Fēizhōu	Africa	朋友 péngyou	friend
遇 yù	to meet	森林 sēnlín	forest	它们 tāmen	they, them (things, animals)
醒 xǐng	to wake up	猩猩 xīngxing	gorilla	生活 shēnghuó	to live
被 bèi	by				

冬冬遇到孙悟空了，后来呢？
Dongdong met the Monkey King, then what happened?

　　后来冬冬醒了。
　　Then Dongdong woke up.
　　他被奶奶叫醒了。
　　He was woken up by his grandma.

啊，他做了一个梦。
Oh, he had a dream.

　　冬冬说，他长大了，要做宇航员。
　　Dongdong says he will be an astronaut when he grows up.
　　玛丽，你长大了做什么？
　　What do you want to be when you grow up, Mary?

我长大了去非洲森林。
I want to go to the forests in Africa when I grow up.

　　为什么去非洲森林？
　　Why do you want to go to the forests in Africa?

我要跟大猩猩做朋友，
I want to make friends with the gorillas,
看看它们怎么生活。
and see how they live.

　　芳子呢？
　　What about Fangzi?

芳子想做一个老师，
Fangzi wants to be a teacher,
教小朋友《新儿童汉语》。
and teachs her pupils *New Chinese for Children*.

Dōngdong yùdào Sūn Wùkōng le, hòulái ne?

　　Hòulái Dōngdong xǐng le.

　　Tā bèi nǎinai jiàoxǐng le.

À, tā zuòle yí gè mèng.

　　Dōngdong shuō, tā zhǎng-dà le, yào zuò yǔhángyuán.

　　Mǎlì, nǐ zhǎngdàle zuò shénme?

Wǒ zhǎngdàle qù Fēizhōu sēnlín.

　　Wèi shénme qù Fēizhōu sēnlín?

Wǒ yào gēn dàxīngxing zuò péngyou,

kànkan tāmen zěnme shēnghuó.
　　Fāngzǐ ne?

Fāngzǐ xiǎng zuò yí gè lǎoshī, jiāo xiǎopéngyǒu *Xīn Értóng Hànyǔ*.

Read aloud

冬冬跟孙悟空一起飞。他们飞得真快，快要到月亮了……真可惜，他被奶奶叫醒了。冬冬说，他长大了要做一个宇航员，坐着飞船到月亮上旅行。兰兰说她长大了要做一个大夫。山姆说他要做一个运动员（yùndòngyuán, athlete）。芳子喜欢做老师。她汉语学得很好，她要教很多小朋友学汉语。

小朋友，你长大了做什么呢？你能告诉我吗？

Write sentences about what you see in the pictures

奶奶的眼镜被谁找到了？
_____。

电视被谁关上了？
_____。

伞（sǎn umbrella）被兰兰放在哪儿了？
_____。

小乌龟被山姆送给谁了？
_____。

20 新年好

新年 xīnnián	New Year	旧 jiù	old	新 xīn	new
身体 shēntǐ	body	年 nián	year	一定 yídìng	certainly
健康 jiànkāng	health, healthy	进步 jìnbù	progress	更 gèng	more
快乐 kuàilè	happy, glad				

老师，新年好！
Happy New Year, teacher!

阿姨，新年好！
Happy New Year, aunt!

　小朋友，你们好！
　Happy New Year, children!

祝老师和阿姨身体健康，
Good health to our teacher and aunt.

生活快乐！
A happy life to you!

　谢谢，孩子们。
　Thank you, children.

　旧的一年过去了，
　The old year is over.

　你们进步很大。
　You've made great progress.

　新的一年开始了，
　The new year has started.

　你们都长了一岁，
　You are all a year older.

　你们的进步一定更大。
　You'll certainly make greater progress.

老师，再见！
Goodbye, teacher!

　小朋友，再见！
　Goodbye, children!

Lǎoshī, xīnnián hǎo!

Āyí, xīnnián hǎo!

　Xiǎopéngyǒu, nǐmen hǎo!

Zhù lǎoshī hé āyí shēntǐ jiànkāng,

shēnghuó kuàilè!

　Xièxie, háizi men.

　Jiù de yì nián guòqùle,

　nǐmen jìnbù hěn dà.

　Xīn de yì nián kāishǐle,

　nǐmen dōu zhǎngle yí suì,

　nǐmen dè jìnbù yídìng gèng dà.

Lǎoshī, zàijiàn!

　Xiǎopéngyǒu, zàijiàn!

Read aloud

今天是一月一日，冬冬、玛丽、芳子、山姆和兰兰一起到老师家拜年（bàinián, to pay a new year call）。老师看见他们很高兴，请他们进屋坐。阿姨拿出糖、蛋糕和苹果，让他们吃。

玛丽把贺年片（hèniánpiàn, New Year card）送给老师。她说："谢谢老师，这一年您辛苦（xīnkǔ, to work hard）了。"老师说："你们都是好孩子。你们进步很快，我很高兴。在新的一年里，你们一定学得更好，身体更健康。"

Write sentences about what you see in the pictures

祝_____！

祝你圣诞（Shèngdàn, Christmas）_____！

祝_____！

祝_____！

词汇表
Vocabulary List

A
啊	à	oh
矮	ǎi	short

B
把	bǎ	*preposition showing disposal*
吧	ba	*modal particle*
帮	bāng	to help
北海公园	Běihǎi Gōngyuán	Beihai Park
被	bèi	by
本子	běnzi	exercise book
比	bǐ	to compare, than
病	bìng	to be ill
不用	búyòng	need not

C
擦	cā	to wipe
猜	cāi	to guess
长	cháng	long
长城	Chángchéng	the Great Wall
嫦娥	Cháng'é	Fairy Chang'e
车	chē	vehicle
出	chū	to come out
船	chuán	boat, ship
窗户	chuānghu	window
次	cì	time

D
打电话	dǎ(diànhuà)	to make (a phone call)
打(开)	dǎ(kāi)	to turn on, to open
打针	dǎzhēn	to have an injection
大	dà	big, old
打扫	dǎsǎo	to clean
戴	dài	to wear

大夫	dàifu	doctor
蛋糕	dàngāo	cake
当然	dāngrán	of course
到	dào	to go to, to arrive
等	děng	to wait
第	dì	ordinal prefix (-st, -nd, -rd)
地球	dìqiú	the earth
电车	diànchē	tram
电话	diànhuà	telephone
电视	diànshì	TV
电影	diànyǐng	film
对不起	duìbuqǐ	sorry
多少	duōshao	how much, how many

F

发烧	fāshāo	to have a fever
放	fàng	to put
放(假)	fàng(jià)	to have (a holiday)
飞	fēi	to fly
飞船	fēichuán	spaceship
非洲	Fēizhōu	Africa
复习	fùxí	to review

G

干	gàn	to do
刚才	gāngcái	just now
高	gāo	high
高兴	gāoxìng	happy
告诉	gàosu	to tell
哥哥	gēge	elder brother
给	gěi	for, to
跟	gēn	with
更	gèng	more
功课	gōngkè	lesson
故事	gùshi	story
关	guān	to close
过(来)	guò(lai)	to come (here)
过	guo	*aspectual particle*

H

还	hái	as well; still
还是	háishi	or

海边	hǎi biān	seaside
轰	hōng	boom
后来	hòulái	later
湖	hú	lake
划	huá	to row
回	huí	to go back
火车	huǒchē	train

J

家	jiā	home, family
加	jiā	plus
见	jiàn	to see
健康	jiànkāng	heath, healthy
教室	jiàoshì	classroom
讲	jiǎng	to tell
节目	jiémù	programme
金鱼	jīnyú	goldfish
进	jìn	to come in, to enter
进步	jìnbù	progress
旧	jiù	old

K

开	kāi	to open
开(会)	kāi(huì)	to have (a meeting)
开始	kāishǐ	to begin, to start
咳嗽	késou	to cough
可惜	kěxī	it's a pity
哭	kū	to cry, to weep
块	kuài	*measure word*
快乐	kuàilè	happy, glad

L

老鼠	lǎoshǔ	mouse
礼物	lǐwù	present
俩	liǎ	two, both
练习	liànxí	exercise
旅行	lǚxíng	to travel

M

抹布	mābù	rag

买	mǎi	to buy
忙	máng	busy
毛	máo	*mao*
帽子	màozi	hat
没关系	méi guānxi	that's all right, it doesn't matter
妹妹	mèimei	younger sister
门	mén	door
梦	mèng	dream
明天	míngtiān	tomorrow

N

拿	ná	to hold, to take
奶奶	nǎinai	grandma
能	néng	can, able to
年	nián	year
您	nín	you (polite form, singular)

P

爬	pá	to climb
怕	pà	to be afraid
胖	pàng	fat, chubby
跑	pǎo	to run
朋友	péngyou	friend
票	piào	ticket

Q

钱	qián	money
请	qǐng	please

R

让	ràng	to let

S

赛跑	sàipǎo	to run a race
森林	sēnlín	forest
山	shān	hill
商店	shāngdiàn	shop
上	shàng	to come up
上班	shàngbān	to go to work
身体	shēntǐ	body
生活	shēnghuó	to live

事	shì	thing
售货员	shòuhuòyuán	shop assistant
舒服	shūfu	well, comfortable
暑假	shǔjià	summer holiday, summer vacation
睡觉	shuìjiào	to go to bed
送	sòng	to give (a present), to take sb. to
算	suàn	to reckon, to add up
孙悟空	Sūn Wùkōng	the Monkey King
所以	suǒyǐ	so, therefore

T

它	tā	it
它们	tāmen	they, them (things and animals)
太	tài	too, very
糖	táng	sweets, candy
桃子	táozi	peach
特别	tèbié	special

疼	téng	ache, pain
天	tiān	day
跳	tiào	to jump
跳高	tiàogāo	high jump
听	tīng	to listen

W

完	wán	to finish
忘	wàng	to forget
喂	wèi	hello
为什么	wèi shénme	why
乌龟	wūguī	tortoise

X

下	xià	to get off
小朋友	xiǎopéngyǒu	child, kid
谢谢	xièxie	to thank, thank you
新	xīn	new
新年	xīnnián	New Year
猩猩	xīngxing	gorilla

醒	xǐng	to wake up

Y

呀	ya	*modal particle*
眼镜	yǎnjìng	glasses
要	yào	will, to be going to
药	yào	medicine
爷爷	yéye	grandpa
一定	yídìng	certainly
以前	yǐqián	ago, before
椅子	yǐzi	chair
一点儿	yìdiǎnr	a little
一起	yìqǐ	together
因为	yīnwèi	because, for
用	yòng	to use
宇航员	yǔhángyuán	astronaut
遇	yù	to meet
月亮	yuèliang	the moon
运动会	yùndònghuì	sports meet

Z

咱们	zánmen	we, us
脏	zāng	dirty
怎么	zěnme	how
张	zhāng	*measure word*
长	zhǎng	to grow
找	zhǎo	to look for
着	zhe	*particle indicating continuous action*
祝	zhù	to wish, to congratulate
捉	zhuō	to catch
昨天	zuótiān	yesterday
坐	zuò	to sit

辅导材料

第1课

1．"请进"，"请坐"是比较客气的用语。

2．"他去哪儿了？""爸爸上班了。""妈妈去商店了。"这些句子最后的语气助词"了"，都表示某个事情或情况肯定已经发生。试比较："他去哪儿？"（Where is he going?）"他去哪儿了？"（Where has he gone?）

第2课

"你跳高了吗？""我没有跳高。"回答"……了吗？"的问题，如果答案是否定的，则在动词前用"没有"（或"没"），句尾去掉语气助词"了"。如"她没有跳舞，她唱歌了。""哥哥今天没上班。"

第3课

1．"喂，谁呀？""喂"是打招呼的声音。在打电话或接电话时常用。打电话时通报自己的姓名用"我是……"，询问对方的姓名用"你是……吗"。

2．"你忙不忙？""你能不能来我家？""冬冬来不来？"是将句子谓语中的主要成分（动词或形容词）的肯定形式和否定形式并列起来提问。上述句子的意思跟"你忙吗？""你能来我家吗？""冬冬来吗？"等用"吗"提问是一样的。

注意：动词"有"的肯定形式与否定形式的并列应该是"有没有"。

第4课

"我送你一件礼物。"有一些动词可以带两个宾语。表示"人"的宾语在前，表示"东西"的宾语在后。如"爸爸给我一支笔。""老师教我们算术。"但要注意这种能带两个宾语的动词在汉语中不是很多。

第5课

1．"您给我们讲个故事，好吗？"介词"给"跟它的宾语"我们"组成介词结构，放在动词前作状语。注意：这个句子不能说成"您讲我们一个故事，好吗？"

2．"这个故事我们听过了。""这个，我们也看过电影了。"助词"过"放在动词后边说明某种动作曾在过去发生，用来强调有过这种经历。如"他以前学过汉语。""我吃过中国菜。"

3．"你们喜欢什么呢？"语气助词"呢"用在疑问句的句尾，使全句的语气缓和。带

"吗"的疑问句后不能再加"呢"。

4."我们最喜欢听孙悟空的故事。""孙悟空"是中国古典小说《西游记》中的人物，是中国人民喜爱的具有浪漫主义色彩的英雄形象。

第6课

1."没有去过。""动词+过"的否定形式是"没（有）……过"。如"他以前没有学过汉语。""我没有吃过中国菜。"

2."我在那儿划过船。""星期天你跟我们一起去，好吗？"介词"在"、"跟"等跟它们的宾语组成介词结构，放在动词前作状语。"在"的宾语常是表示处所的。"跟"的宾语如果是指人的名词或代词，常与"一起"连用。如"我在学校打电话。""我跟冬冬一起玩儿。"

第7课

1."不谢。"这是回答别人感谢的用语。

2."北海要到了。""我们要下车了。""要+动词（+宾语）+了"表示动作很快就要发生。如"要下雨了。""现在九点了，冬冬要来了。"

3."您坐这儿吧！"语气助词"吧"用在表示请求、劝告、命令的句子句尾，使整个句子的语气比较缓和。如："我们去吧。""请坐吧。"

第8课

1."我去海边旅行。""我们坐火车去。"在这两个句子里，主语后边都有两个连用的动词（或动词结构）。后一个动词所代表的动作常常是前一动词所代表的动作的目的（"去海边旅行"），或者前一动词所代表的动作是后一动词所代表的动作的方式（"坐火车去"）。

2."这是第一次。"序数的表示方法是在数词前加"第"。如"第一"、"第二"、"第十二"等。

第9课

1."咱们"是口语中常用的一个词，它包括谈话的对方；而"我们"则一般不包括谈话的对方。如"我们去北海，你去吗？""咱们一起去，好吗？"

2."咱们打扫打扫，好么？"动词重叠使用常表示动作经历的时间短促，或表示轻松、随便，有时也表示尝试。如："我想想。""我听听。""你到我家来玩儿玩儿吧。"

第10课

1."咱们俩比一比"。"俩"是口语中常用的词，就是"两个"的意思。常说"我们俩"，"你们俩"，"他们俩"。"比一比"就是"比比"。单音节动词重叠，中间可以加

"一"。如："我想一想。""我听一听。"

2．"我比你高。""你比冬冬矮一点儿。"介词"比"可以用来表示比较。其词序是："名词或代词+比+另一名词或代词+形容词"。如："这个教室比那个教室脏。""妈妈比爸爸忙。"

如果要表示比较的结果差别不大，可以在形容词后加上"一点儿"或"点儿"。如："他比我早一点儿。""今天比昨天冷点儿。"

3．"我胖还是冬冬胖？"用连词"还是"连接两种可能的答案，由回答的人来选择，这也是一种提问的方式。如："咱们划船还是爬山？""他是中国人还是日本人？"

第11课

1．"山姆，下来！下来！""你上来吧。""你快点儿出来。"有些动词后边常用"来"表示动作朝着说话人所在地。如"请进来吧！""他跑来了。""过来，我看看。"

2．"我的小狗捉了一只大老鼠。""了"加在动词后边表示动作的完成。如"他买了三张票。""老爷爷讲了孙悟空的故事。"注意：动词带"了"以后，它的宾语前边一般要带数量词或其他定语。

第12课

1．"他让我等他。"这类句子的前一个动词常带有使令的意义。它的宾语又是后一个动词的主语。如"他请我去他家。""我让他上来。"

2．"咱们进去看看吧。"动词后边加"去"表示动作离开说话人所在地。如"冬冬在山上呢，咱们也上去吧。""玛丽下去了吗？"

第13课

1．"你好，小朋友。""小朋友"是对儿童的一种称呼。

2．"一块一加一块二是两块三"。中国的人民币的计算单位是"块（kuài）、毛（máo）、分（fēn）"。一块等于十毛，一毛等于十分。

3"对不起"是表示道歉的用语。回答常用"没关系"。

第14课

"她哪儿不舒服？""她头痛。"在这两个句子里"哪儿不舒服"、"头痛"是谓语，用来说明主语的。而这两个谓语本身又是主谓结构。又如："他汉语很好。""我学习很忙。"

第15课

"我复习完了。"动词"复习"只表示"review"这个动作。在"复习"后边加补语

"完"，则表示复习这个动作有了结果（to finish reviewing）。同样，在"找"(to look for)和"找到"(to find)，"放"(to put)和"放在"(to put some where)以及前面学过的"看"(to look at)和"看见"(to see)等几组词语中，前者都只表示动作，后者则表示动作有了结果。注意：这种句子用"没有"否定。如"没有复习完"，"没有找到"，"没有看见"等。

第 16 课

1．"你把电视打开。""你把电视关上。"这类带有介词"把"的句子，用来强调说明某些动作对事物的处置及处置的结果。这种句子的词序是："名词或代词+把+名词或代词（被处置的事物）+动词+其他成分（如动作的结果）"。例如："请你把门开开。""我要把算术做完。"

2．"写对"、"打开"、"关上"也是表示动作有了结果。

第 17 课

1．"他们身上穿着什么呢？""他们头上戴着特别的帽子。"动词后面加上助词"着"，表示动作或动态的持续。如"电视开着吗？""桌上放着本子和笔。"

2．"他们要看看嫦娥和小白兔。"嫦娥是中国神话中从人间飞到月亮上的仙女。传说月亮中还有一只玉兔。

第 18 课

"因为它很长，所以叫长城。""因为"、"所以"这两个连词可以同时用在一个句子中，也可以只用其中一个。如："她病了，所以今天不能到学校。""我帮奶奶找眼镜，因为她眼睛不太好。"

第 19 课

"他被奶奶叫醒了。"这类带介词"被"的句子用来表示主语和动词的被动关系。其词序是："名词或代词（受事）+被+名词或代词（施事)+动词+其他成分（如动作的结果）。"如："电视被她关上了。""我的书被妈妈找到了。"注意：并不是所有表示被动意思的句子都要用"被"。只有当强调这种被动关系或是要指出施事者时，才用"被"字句。不用"被"也可以表示被动的意思。如："电视关上了。""我的书找到了。"

第 20 课

1．"新年好"是新年时表示祝福的用语。

2．"你们的进步一定更大。""更"是表示程度的副词，常用在形容词、动词前面表示更高的程度。如"更新"、"更喜欢"、"更想"等。

Teacher's Notes

Lesson One

1. 请进 and 请坐 are expressions used to make polite requests.

2. In sentences like 他去哪儿了, 爸爸上班了, and 妈妈去商店了, the modal particle 了 is used to indicate that the event referred to has already taken place. Compare 他去哪儿 (where is he going) with 他去哪儿了 (where has he gone).

Lesson Two

The negative answer to questions with … 了吗？(e.g., 你跳高了吗？) is formed by putting the adverb 没有 (or 没) before the verb and dropping the 了 at the end of the sentence, as in 我没有跳高. More examples: 她没有跳舞, 她唱歌了. 哥哥今天没上班.

Lesson Three

1. 喂 is used to express an informal greeting, and is often used when making or receiving phone calls. In a telephone conversation, 我是… is used to tell the other person one's name; while 你是…吗？or 谁呀？is used to ask who the other person is.

In 谁呀, 呀 is a modal particle.

2. Besides questions with 吗, there are also affirmative-negative questions made by juxtaposing the affirmative and negative forms of the predicative verb or adjective, e.g., 你忙不忙？你能不能来我家？(These questions have the same meaning as 你忙吗？你能来我家吗？)

Note that affirmative-negative questions with the verb 有 should be… 有没有…

Lesson Four

Some verbs can take two objects, with object referring to a person preceding the one referring to a thing, e.g., 我送你一件礼物. 爸爸给我一支笔. 老师教我们算术. Note that there are only a small number of verbs in Chinese that can take two objects.

Lesson Five

1. "Will you please tell us a story?" cannot be expressed in a Chinese sentence like 您讲我们一个故事, 好吗？for the verb 讲 cannot take two objects. The preposition 给 should be used in this case together with its object 我们 and be placed before the main verb 讲, e.g., 您给我们讲个故事, 好吗？(Here 给我们 means "for us".)

For the same reason, it is not correct to say 我打电话他了. The correct form is 我给他打电话了.

2. The aspectual particle 过 placed immediately after a verb denotes that some action took place in the past. 过 is often used to express past experience, e.g., 这个故事我们听过了. 这个我们也看过电影了. 他以前学过汉语. 我们吃过中国菜.

3. The modal particle 呢 is often added to the end of a question to soften its tone, e.g., 你们喜欢听什么呢？However, it is not used in questions with the particle 吗.

4. 孙悟空 (the Monkey King), a romantic and heroic character in the 16th century Chinese novel *Journey to the West,* is well-known and loved by the Chinese.

Lesson Six

1. The negative form of verb + 过 is 没有 + verb + 过, e.g., 没有去过. 他以前没有学过汉语. 我没有吃过中国菜.

2. The preposition 在 and 跟 etc., used with their objects are often placed before verbs as adverbial modifiers. The object of 在 usually refers to places, e.g., 我在那儿划过船. 我在学校打电话. If the object of 跟 is a noun or pronoun referring to a person, it is often used with 一起, e.g., 星期天你跟我们一起去, 好吗？我跟冬冬一起玩儿.

Lesson Seven

1. 不谢 is a reply to 谢谢.

2. The structure 要 + verb (+ object) + 了 indicates that an action is going to take place, e.g., 要下雨了. 现在九点了. 冬冬要来了. 北海要到了. 我们要下车了.

3. The modal particle 吧 can be put at the end of a request, advice or a command to soften the tone of the sentence, e.g., 您坐这儿吧！我们去吧. 请坐吧.

Lesson Eight

1. If the subject of a sentence is followed by two verbal constructions, the second construction sometimes denotes the purpose of the action expressed by the first, as in 我去海边旅行, or the first verb can describe the manner of the action expressed by the second, as in 我们坐火车去.

2. The ordinals are formed by putting 第 before the cardinals, e.g., 第一, 第二, 第十二, etc.

Lesson Nine

1. 咱们 is often used in colloquial speech. It refers to both the speaker and the person spoken to, while 我们 does not often include the person spoken to, e.g., 我们去北海, 你去吗？咱们一起去, 好吗？

2. The reduplication of a verb denoting action indicates that the action is of very short duration, and it makes the action sound less rigid or less formal; sometimes it implies that what is done is just for the purpose of trying something out, e.g., 我想想. 我听听. 你到我家来玩儿玩儿吧, 咱们打扫打扫, 好吗？

Lesson Ten

1. In 咱们俩比一比, the word 俩 means 两个. It is often used in colloquial speech, e.g., 我们俩, 你们俩, 他们俩.

比一比 is the same as 比比. The reduplication of the monosyllabic verb can also be formed with 一 inserted in between, e.g., 我想一想, 我听一听.

2. The preposition 比 is used to compare things following this pattern: noun or pronoun + 比 + another noun or pronoun + adjective, e.g., 我比你高. 这个教室比那个教室脏. 妈妈比爸爸忙. In 你比冬冬矮一点, 一点 or 点儿 is used after the adjective to indicate that the difference between the two things is slight, e.g., 他比我早一点儿. 今天比昨天冷点儿.

3. In a choice-type question the two possible choices can be joined by 还是, e.g., 我胖还是

冬冬胖？咱们划船还是爬山？他是中国人还是日本人？

Lesson Eleven

1. Some verbs are often followed by the directional verb 来 to indicate movement towards the speaker or the thing referred to, e.g., 山姆，下来！下来 (come down)! 你上来吧 (come up). 你快点儿出来 (come out), 请进来吧 (come in)! 他跑来了 (He is running towards us). 过来 (come over here)，我看看.

2. The aspectual particle 了 is used after certain verbs to indicate the completion of the action, e.g., 我的小狗捉了一只大老鼠，他买了三张票，老爷爷讲了孙悟空的故事. Note that the object of a verb with the aspectual particle 了 is usually modified by a numeral-measure word or another attributive.

Lesson Twelve

1. In sentences like 他让我等他, the first verb is often a causative verb such as 请, or 让 and its object is also the subject of the following verb. More examples: 他请我去他家，我他让上来.

2. The directional verb 去 added to some verbs indicates the moving away of the action from the speaker or the thing referred to, e.g., 咱们进去看看吧. 冬冬在上山呢，咱们也上去吧. 玛丽下去了吗？

Lesson Thirteen

1. 小朋友 is used as an address to a child, e.g., 你好，小朋友.
2. The counting units of Renminbi (Chinese currency) are 块 (*kuai*), 毛 (*mao*), 分 (*fen*). One 块 is equal to ten 毛, and one 毛 to ten 分.
3. 对不起 is an expression of apology, meaning "I'm sorry" and the reply to it is usually 没关系.

Lesson Fourteen

In sentences like 她哪儿不舒服 and 她头痛, the predicates 哪儿不舒服 and 头痛 are formed by the subject-predicate construction. More examples: 他汉语很好，我学习很忙.

Lesson Fifteen

In the sentence 我复习完了，the verb 复习 only refers to the action of "reviewing", but by adding the verb 完 as a suffix, the result of 复习 is expressed (to finish reviewing). Similar usages are 找 (to look for) and 找到 (to find), 放 (to put) and 放在 (to put in a place) and 看 (to look at) and 看见 (to see). The second verb in each pair of verbs indicates the result of the first verb. Note that sentences of this type are made negative by placing 没有 before the two verbs, e.g., 我没有复习完. 她没有找到眼镜. 冬冬没有看见他.

Lesson Sixteen

1. In the sentences 你把电视打开 and 你把电视关上, the preposition 把 is used to emphasize how a thing or person is acted upon and the result of this, such as the changing of a position,

the altering of a state, or influence of an action. The structure of this type of sentence is: noun or pronoun (subject) + 把 + noun or pronoun (acted upon) + verb + other elements (such as the result of the action).

More examples: 请你把门开开. 我要把算术作完.

2. The verb constructions 写对, 打开 and 关上 also express that the action of 写, 打 or 关 has achieved its result.

Lesson Seventeen

1. In 他们身上穿着什么呢 and 他们头上戴着特别的帽子, the particle 着 is added to the verb to indicate the continuation of the action or the state. More examples: 电视开着吗？桌上放着本子和笔.

2. 嫦娥 is a fairy in Chinese legend who flew to the moon from the earth. According to the tale, there is also a white rabbit on the moon.

Lesson Eighteen

The conjunctions 因为 and 所以 are either used in a single sentence or separately, e.g., 因为它很长, 所以叫长城. 她病了, 所以今天不能到学校. 我帮奶奶找眼镜, 因为她眼睛不太好.

Lesson Nineteen

In the sentence 他被奶奶叫醒了, the preposition 被 is used to express the passive relationship between the subject and the verb. The structure of this type of sentence is: noun or pronoun (recipient) + 被 + noun or pronoun (performer) + verb + other elements (such as the result of the action), e.g., 电视被他关了. 我的书被妈妈找到了.

Note that not all passive sentences are constructed with 被. 被 is used only when the passive relationship between the subject and the verb is emphasized, or when the performer of the action is indicated. In Chinese a passive sentence can be formed without 被, e.g., 电视关上了. 我的书找到了.

Lesson Twenty

1. 新年好 is a New Year greeting.

2. 更 is an adverb of degree, often used before an adjective or a verb to imply a higher degree, as in 你们的进步一定更大. More examples: 更新, 更喜欢, 更想.

图 书 推 荐
Recommended Titles

快乐儿童汉语 (全两册)
Fun Chinese for Children (2 volumes)

汉英 Chinese-English edition
208 × 275mm，92pp/each
ISBN 9787800529276
ISBN 9787800529283
￥46.00 each

- 适合以英语为母语的学龄前儿童学习汉语的初级读本，共两册，第一册17课，第二册21课。
- 从汉语拼音开始学汉语，形式活泼，语言生动，图文并茂，好学好说，即学即用，学一句可以用一句。
- Elementary readers and textbooks for non-native speaking children to learn Chinese as a foreign language.
- This series consists of 2 volumes. The first includes 17 lessons, and the second 21 lessons.
- Starting from pinyin. Detailed descriptions of tones are given.
- Using dialogues applicable to children's everyday life.
- Games and funny cartoons are provided.

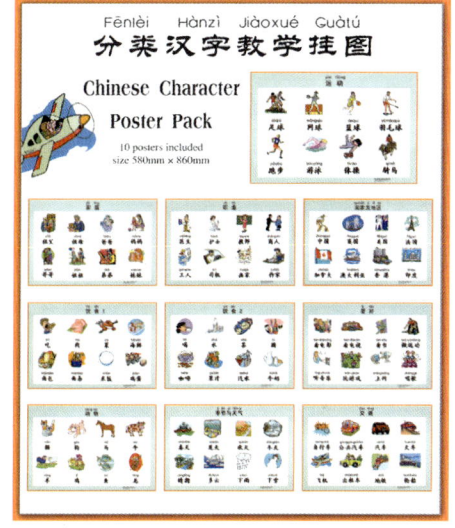

分类汉字教学挂图
Chinese Character Poster Pack
(10 posters)

580 × 860mm each
ISBN 9787802002982
￥118.00

- 《分类汉字教学挂图》共10张，包含国家及地区、职业、交通、爱好、家庭、动物、季节与天气、饮食、运动等最基本的汉字和注音。
- Includes ten posters on countries and regions, occupations, vehicles, hobbies, family members, animals, seasons and weather, food and sport.
- All the words are illustrated. The posters can be used to decorate classrooms.

责任编辑：韩　颖
英　　译：张　耘
封面设计：王新乐
印刷监制：佟汉冬

图书在版编目（CIP）数据

新儿童汉语 · 3 ／ 刘珣，张亚军，丁永寿编著 . —— 北京：华语教学出版社，2011
ISBN 978-7-5138-0084-6

Ⅰ. ①新… Ⅱ. ①刘… ②张… ③丁… Ⅲ. ①汉语－对外汉语教学－儿童教育－教材
Ⅳ. ① H195.4

中国版本图书馆 CIP 数据核字 (2011) 第 098549 号

新儿童汉语 · 3

刘珣　张亚军　丁永寿 编著
*
© 华语教学出版社
华语教学出版社出版
（中国北京百万庄大街 24 号　邮政编码　100037）
电话 :(86)10-68320585, 68997826
传真 :(86)10-68997826, 68326333
网址：www.sinolingua.com.cn
电子信箱：hyjx@sinolingua.com.cn
三河市汇鑫印务有限公司印刷
2011 年（16 开）第 1 版
（汉英）
ISBN 978-7-5138-0084-6
定价：49.00 元